D1061395

Cotton Candy Machines

Charlotte Hunter

rourkeeducationalmedia.com

Scan for Related Titles and Teacher Resources

Before & After Reading Activities

Level: **P**

Teaching Focus: 3-2-1 Strategy

The 3-2-1 strategy involves writing about three things students discovered, two things they found interesting, and one question they still have after reading the book.

Before Reading:

Building Academic Vocabulary and Background Knowledge

Before reading a book, it is important to set the stage for your child or student by using pre-reading strategies. This will help them develop their vocabulary, increase their reading comprehension, and make connections across the curriculum.

1. *Read the title and look at the cover. Let's make predictions about what this book will be about.*
2. *Take a picture walk by talking about the pictures/photographs in the book. Implant the vocabulary as you take the picture walk. Be sure to talk about the text features such as headings, the Table of Contents, glossary, bolded words, captions, charts/diagrams, or index.*
3. *Have students read the first page of text with you then have students read the remaining text.*
4. *Strategy Talk – use to assist students while reading.*
   - *Get your mouth ready*
   - *Look at the picture*
   - *Think…does it make sense*
   - *Think…does it look right*
   - *Think…does it sound right*
   - *Chunk it – by looking for a part you know*
5. *Read it again.*
6. *After reading the book, complete the activities below.*

Content Area Vocabulary
Use glossary words in a sentence.

crystals
engineering
force
rotations
strands
technology

After Reading:

Comprehension and Extension Activity

After reading the book, work on the following questions with your child or students in order to check their level of reading comprehension and content mastery.

1. *Does the color of the flossugar you use change the color of the cotton candy? (Inferring)*
2. *What happens to the sugar crystals when they melt? (Asking questions)*
3. *Who invented the first cotton candy machine? (Text to self connection)*
4. *What is another name used for cotton candy? (Summarize)*

Extension Activity

Make your own cotton candy picture! You will need: Shaving cream, glue, a paintbrush, red and blue food coloring, a marker, paper, and scissors. Start by free-drawing a cotton candy shape on a piece of paper. Then mix half glue with shaving cream until it forms peaks. Add the red and blue food coloring so you make pretty cotton candy colors. Cut out the cotton candy shape and start painting swirls with both colors! Cut out a cone shape for the handle piece. It should stay puffy for about a day or two then start getting flat. Make sure you let it dry before touching it!

Table of Contents

Sweet Treat

Have you ever eaten cotton candy?

Before the cotton candy machine was invented, spun sugar was expensive to create.

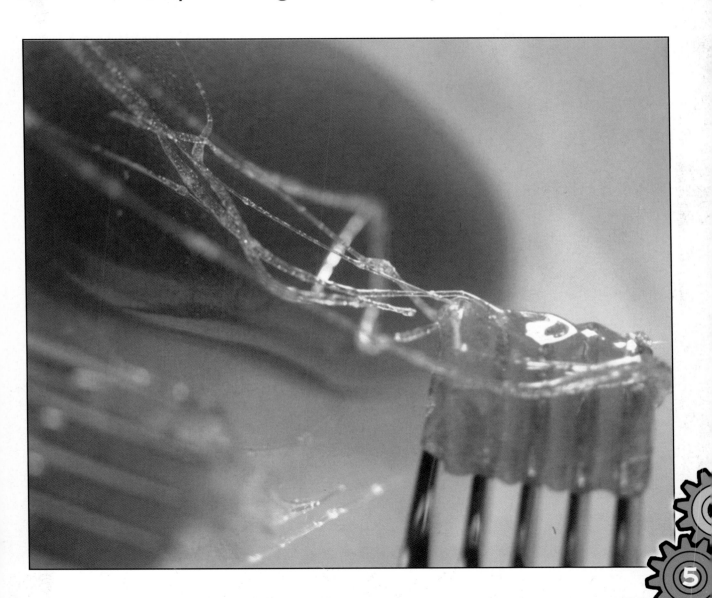

A New Spin

Hundreds of years ago, sugar was heated, then spun with a fork to make an early form of cotton candy. It took a long time, and cost a lot of money.

The first electric cotton candy machine was invented in 1897 by William Morrison and John C. Wharton. William was a dentist!

Not long ago, **technology** and **engineering** made this sweet treat easy to make, so anyone could enjoy it.

Making Cotton Candy

How does a cotton candy machine work?

Colorful, flavored sugar is poured in the center of the cotton candy machine in a spinning head.

The special sugar, called flossugar, is warmed up to 300 degrees Fahrenheit (149 degrees Celsius) by heaters at the top of the head.

head

The sugar quickly begins to melt. The solid sugar **crystals** become a liquid syrup.

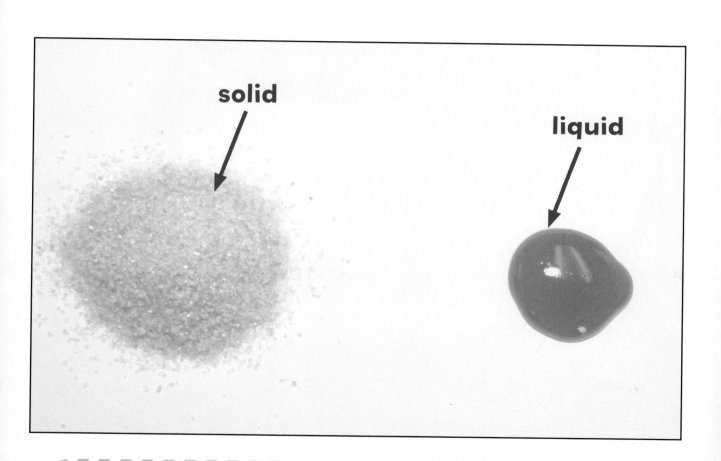

solid

liquid

Cotton candy is also known as Fairy Floss.

The head spins at 3,400 **rotations** per minute.

As the head spins, centrifugal **force** pushes the melted sugar through tiny holes in the head.

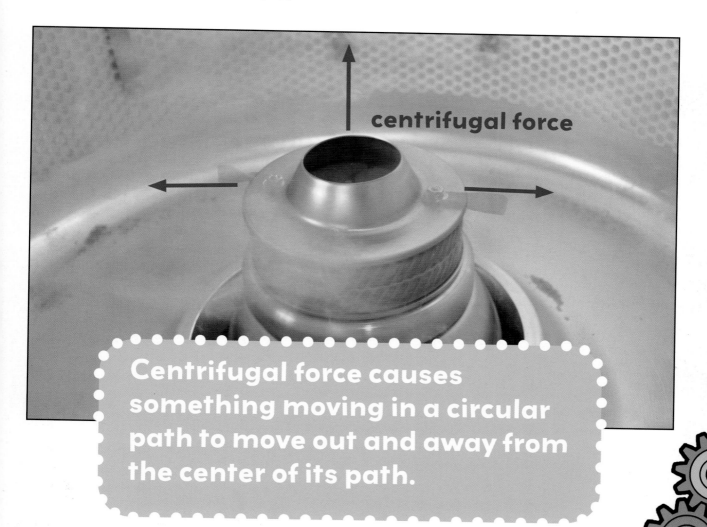

centrifugal force

Centrifugal force causes something moving in a circular path to move out and away from the center of its path.

As the syrup is pushed out of the head away from the heat, it is quickly cooled by the air.

As it cools, the sugar turns back into a solid. But now, instead of solid sugar crystals, the sugar is spun into fluffy **strands**.

The strands are similar to cotton fibers. That's how cotton candy got its name!

The soft, airy strands are caught in a bowl that surrounds the spinning head.

After a few minutes, the strands build up in the bowl.

When enough of the fluffy treat is in the bowl, the machine operator spins a stick around the edges.

The cotton candy winds around the stick.

Then, it's ready to eat!

Photo Glossary

 **crystals** (KRIS-tuhls): Crystals are substance that form a pattern of many flat surfaces. Sugar crystals are shaped like tiny cubes.

 **engineering** (en-juh-NEER-ing): Engineerin is the process of designing and building machines or structures.

 **force** (fors): In science terms, force is any action that produces, stops, or changes the shape or movement of an object.

 **rotations** (ro-TAY-shuns): When something spins around an axis or center, it is making rotations.

 **strands** (strands): Things that look like a thread are called strands. Cotton candy is made of many strands of sugar glass.

 **technology** (tek-NAH-luh-jee): Technology is the use of science and engineering to do practical things. Technology aims to make everyday life easier.

Index

Websites to Visit

www.enchantedlearning.com/inventors/page/c/cottoncandy.shtml

http://wonderopolis.org/wonder/who-invented-cotton-candy

www.candyhistory.net/candy-origin/cotton-candy-history

About the Author

Charlotte Hunter is a writer, editor, and mother of four in Tampa, Florida. She looks forward to the state fair every year, and loves to watch cotton candy sellers spin their tasty sweets. She thinks nothing smells quite as wonderful as a fresh batch of cotton candy.

Meet The Author!
www.meetREMauthors.com

© 2017 Rourke Educational Media

All rights reserved. No part of this book may be reproduced or utilized in any form or by any means, electronic or mechanical including photocopying, recording, or by any information storage and retrieval system without permission in writing from the publisher.

www.rourkeeducationalmedia.com

PHOTO CREDITS: Cover © Darren Mower, Mr. PONGPIT PANGLAO; Title Page © Just2shutter; p. 4 © RainerPlendi; p.5 © Studio Adna www.fotosearch.com; p.7 © Andy Gehrig; p.8 © Nostalgia Products; p.9-13,17 © Rhea Magaro; p. 15 © BallBall14; p.16 © jeffhochstrasser; p.18 © Rossosiena; p.19 © Americanspirit; p. 20 Kuruneko; p.21 © ktaylorg

Edited by: Keli Sipperley
Cover and Interior Design by: Jen Thomas

Cotton Candy Machines / Charlotte Hunter
(How It Works)
ISBN 978-1-68191-687-3 (hard cover)(alk. paper)
ISBN 978-1-68191-788-7 (soft cover)
ISBN 978-1-68191-887-7 (e-Book)
Library of Congress Control Number: 2016932564

Printed in the United States of America, North Mankato, Minnesota

Library of Congress PCN Data

Also Available as:

ROURKE'S
e-Books